COUNTRY EXPLORERS

JAMAICA

Michael Capek

⌐ Lerner Publications Company • Minneapolis

Lerner Publications Company
A division of Lerner Publishing Group, Inc.
241 First Avenue North
Minneapolis, MN 55401 U.S.A.

Website address: www.lernerbooks.com

Library of Congress Cataloging-in-Publication Data

Capek, Michael.
    Jamaica / by Michael Capek.
    p.   cm. — (Country explorers)
    Includes index.
    ISBN 978–1–58013–604–4 (lib. bdg. : alk. paper)
    1. Jamaica—Juvenile literature. I. Title.
F1868.2.C38 2010
972.92—dc22   2009019480

Manufactured in the United States of America
1 – VI – 12/15/09

Table of Contents

Welcome!

We're going to Jamaica! The island of Jamaica sits in the Caribbean Sea. That's part of the Atlantic Ocean. It is easy to spot Jamaica on a map. Find the island of Cuba. It lies south of the state of Florida. Can you find the island that sits to the south of Cuba? You have found Jamaica!

The island of Jamaica is surrounded by the beautiful waters of the Caribbean Sea.

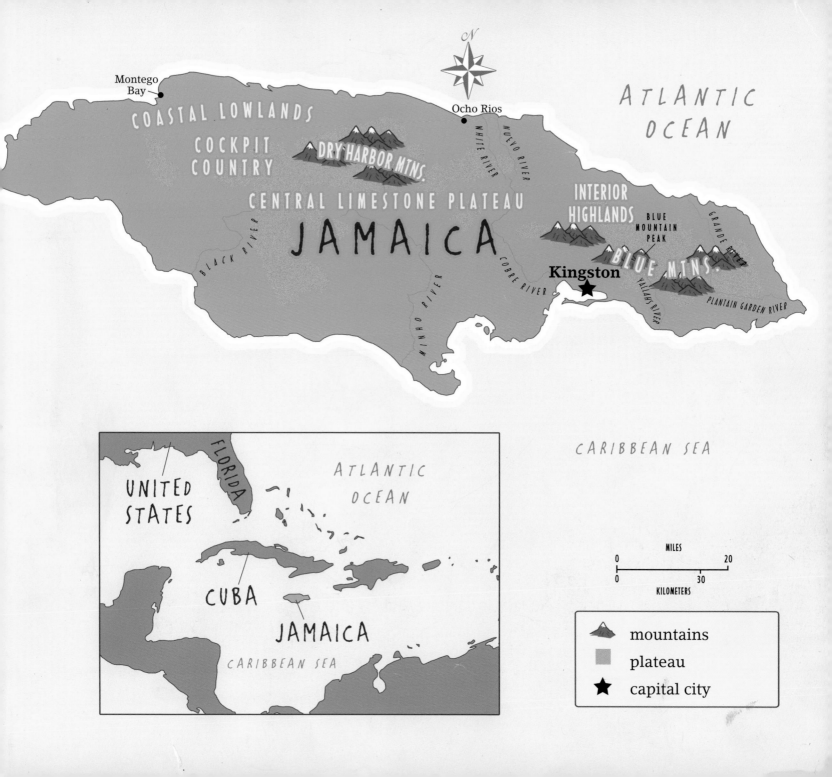

Wet and Wild

Lots of rain falls in Jamaica. Rivers and creeks cut through the island. Many waterways plunge down slopes to waterfalls. Kids love to splash in them.

Crocodiles float in the water too. They swim next to boats. People in the boats might feed snacks to the crocodiles. But watch your toes! Crocodile teeth are sharp.

Map Whiz Quiz

Take a look at the map on page 5. Trace the outline of Jamaica onto a sheet of paper. Can you find the Blue Mountains? Color them blue! Can you find Cockpit Country? Color it green!

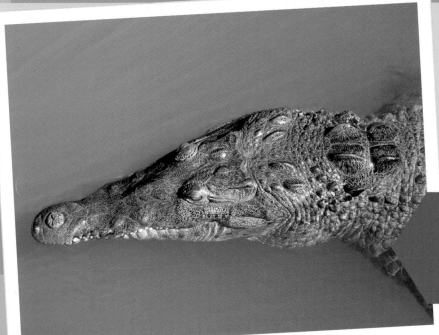

Crocodiles are a common site in part of Jamaica. This croc is swimming in the Black River.

Across the Island

Sandy beaches cover most of Jamaica. But in some spots, the Caribbean Sea meets high cliffs. Fishing boats steer into the ports along the island's coast. Flat plains separate the coast from Jamaica's mountain ranges. The Blue Mountains rise on the eastern side of the island. Jamaica's tallest mountain, Blue Mountain Peak, pokes into the clouds.

In the west, Cockpit Country lies in a wet limestone forest. Its hills and valleys attract giant butterflies.

Cockpit Country (*left*) and cliffs giving way to sandy beaches are beautiful sights in Jamaica.

Warm Weather

If you go to Jamaica, bring your shorts and T-shirts! Jamaica has a tropical climate. This means the weather is hot and humid (wet).

These children and their mother enjoy a day at the beach.

Banana plants and coconut palms grow well in this weather. They blanket the island's mountains all year. Wind blows into Jamaica from the ocean. Jamaicans call the wind the Doctor Breeze. It makes people feel better on hot days.

Early Days

For hundreds of years, only the Arawak Indians lived in Jamaica. Spaniards arrived in the early 1500s. They forced the Arawaks to work for them. Many Arawaks died from overwork and Spanish illnesses. The Spaniards then brought Africans to work as slaves.

These Africans were brought to Jamaica as slaves to work in sugarcane fields.

This drawing shows the Maroons, a group of former slaves. They are waiting to attack slaveholders during fighting in the late 1700s.

In 1655, the British took over Jamaica. They brought more people from Africa. Some slaves escaped. Many joined the Maroons, a group of former slaves. The Maroons lived in Jamaica's hills and mountains. The Maroons fought against the slaveholders. Finally, the British freed the slaves in 1834.

The Jamaicans

A favorite Jamaican saying is, "Out of many, one people." Most Jamaicans trace their families to Africa.

These Jamaican children are of African descent.

Others have relatives from Europe or Asia. Lots of Jamaicans have relatives from two or more continents. But the people who live on the island are proud to be Jamaicans.

This Jamaican man sells fruits and vegetables on the beach. Some Jamaicans have European ancestors.

Big City

Kingston is Jamaica's capital. The city rests on the southern coast near the Blue Mountains. About one out of three Jamaicans lives in Kingston. Huge ships arrive in its port. Taxis, buses, and people crowd the roads. On every corner, music blares from radios.

Families live in brightly painted apartment buildings. They are squeezed among restaurants, churches, and shops. Pet pigs, cats, and dogs roam the streets. Imagine that!

People and cars share a busy street in Montego Bay in northwestern Jamaica.

Family Ties

In Jamaica, most families are big. Moms and dads often have three or more kids. Aunts, uncles, grandmas, and grandpas usually live nearby.

This family walks along a bridge in Jamaica.

Most babies in Jamaica are taken care of by their mothers or other female family members.

Family members like to help one another. Moms are in charge of raising their kids. But grandmas and aunts pitch in too. "Aunties" take care of lots of kids. The aunties are not related to the kids. They are good friends of the family.

Bananas are grown on this large farm in Jamaica.

Shopping

Most Jamaican families live in the countryside. They grow yams, beans, and breadfruit on small farms. Breadfruit is a round or oval fruit. The inside looks and feels like bread.

Farmers sell their extra food at open-air markets in towns. Some merchants spread their goods on the sidewalk. They set high prices. Shoppers bargain to get a good deal. That is part of the fun!

This Jamaican man sells fruit at a stand in a city on the northeastern coast.

Patois

English is Jamaica's official language. Kids speak English in school. But most Jamaicans speak patois on the streets and at home. Patois sounds like English spoken with a Jamaican accent (way of talking).

Dear Holly,

Jamaica is like a warm, green garden. This morning was sunny. We walked in a field full of huge golden butterflies. They were bigger than my hand. Later, it began to rain. Auntie found a giant banana leaf to use as an umbrella! Walk Good! (That is how Jamaicans say good-bye.)

Grace

You
You
Anyw

Jamaica

This family enjoys talking at a restaurant in Jamaica.

Speak Patois (pah-TWAH)!

Here are some patois expressions. Try them out on your friends. Can they understand you?

boonoonoonoos	boo-NOO-noo-noose	beautiful
cool runnings	KOOL RON-nings	greetings
nyam	NEE-yahm	eat
yenky	YAIN-kee	thank you

Celebrate

Jamaicans love to celebrate! Music festivals bring fans together. Both famous musicians and beginners perform.

These women and girls dance at a festival in Kingston, Jamaica.

24

Some festivals mark religious holidays, such as Christmas or Easter. Carnival takes place before Lent, a time of fasting and prayer. Jonkonnu is a favorite festival at Christmastime. To celebrate, folks wear masks and costumes. The outfits are wild!

A dancer takes part in a parade during Carnival in Jamaica. Many Jamaicans celebrate in the days before Lent begins.

Getting There

What is bright purple or shiny red and zooms or crawls? A bus in Jamaica! The buses might be early or late. Jamaican riders squish on anyway.

Other Jamaicans ride trains, bikes, or mopeds. Some drift on rafts. Take off your shoes before you get on. Rafts get pretty wet. And watch out for the places where the water flows fast!

Jamaicans use bikes (*far left*), rafts, and other kinds of transportation to get around.

Tourists relax on the deck of a cruise ship parked in a port on the coast of Jamaica.

Pirates

Long ago, pirates sailed the Caribbean Sea. They stole treasure from other ships. Some even stole whole ships from their victims. Where did the pirates hide out? On the island of Jamaica! These days, ships bring travelers and goods instead of stolen treasure.

Game Time

Whack! A ball goes flying, and the crowd goes wild. Fans are cheering, singing, dancing, and drumming. What is going on? You are at a cricket game! Cricket is a little bit like baseball. It is Jamaica's favorite sport.

Cricket is a popular sport in many of the countries in the Caribbean.

Running is a popular sport too. Jamaican athletes have won medals for their speed at the Olympics.

Jamaicans also enjoy playing dominoes *(right)*. Youngsters and old folks alike play against one another in this game.

Time for School

Jamaican kids start school when they turn six years old. They learn reading, writing, and math. Jamaican schools are crowded. Kids have to share books and desks. In fact, so many kids go to school that they must also share school days. Half the students go to school in the morning. Half go in the afternoon.

These students are taking a test in their classroom in Ocho Rios, Jamaica.

A teacher writes on the blackboard at a school on the northern coast of Jamaica.

All Dressed Up

On school days, students dress in tidy uniforms. Girls wear shirts with skirts or jumpers. Boys dress in shirts and pants.

These girls go to school in Kingston.

Jamaican men usually dress in pants and shirts. Women choose comfortable dresses. It is so hot in Jamaica that lots of kids prefer swimsuits or shorts when they're not in school.

When not in school, kids dress to stay cool.

33

Art

Jamaican artists carve beautiful wooden sculptures. Their style springs partly from their African heritage. But European wood carving has also affected Jamaican style.

A wood-carver works at his craft (*left*). Many carvings can be found in Jamaican shops (*above*).

34

Other artists use bright paints to make small pictures or huge murals. Many Jamaican artists like their work to look Jamaican.

This colorful mural decorates a building in Ocho Rios.

Dub Poetry

Dub poetry is popular in Jamaica. Dub poetry is a little like rap music. Dub poems have a strong rhythm. The poets speak in patois. Drums and music often play in the background. Jamaicans love to watch poets perform.

Drummers or other musicians sometimes play with dub poets.

Some dub poets tell old Jamaican folktales. Others read new poems about hard times or happy events. Huge crowds come to watch dub poets perform. They do not just watch! The fans shout, clap, and drum along with the poet.

Anansi!

Some dub poets tell stories about Anansi. He is a magic spider. He tricks other animals that are larger or that think they are more clever than he is. Anansi stories came to Jamaica with the slaves from Africa.

Many Jamaicans like to dance and sing along at concerts and festivals.

Reggae Beat

Jamaicans love reggae music. Musicians bang drums, strum electric guitars, and sing in patois. Fans across the world love reggae too. Most reggae songs are about peace and love.

Reggae musician Bob Marley came from Jamaica. He was famous all over the world.

Bob Marley

Bob Marley is Jamaica's most famous reggae star. The house where he once lived has become a popular museum. A statue of the singer greets visitors outside.

Religion

Most Jamaicans are Christians. The Spanish and British shared their religion with their African slaves. Many Jamaicans combine Christianity with other religions that have African roots.

These girls go to a Christian church in Kingston, Jamaica.

Some Jamaicans are Rastafarians. This faith began in Jamaica. Rastafarians are vegetarians. They do not eat meat. They preach love and peace. Rastafarians are easy to spot! That is because they wear their hair in long, thick twists called dreadlocks.

This man shows off his long dreadlocks.

Barbecue Time

Nyam! Remember that word? It is patois for "eat." Long ago, Jamaicans came up with a way to cook what they called *barbacoa*. They covered meat with a spicy sauce. Then they dug holes in the ground. They built wood fires in the pits. Finally, they roasted the meat over the open fire.

This Jamaican meal has grilled chicken, grilled corn on the cob, some fruits, vegetables, and rice.

These days, Jamaicans call barbacoa barbecue. And most Jamaicans barbecue on grills instead of in pits. In Jamaican cities and towns, it is easy to find a barbecue stall. Look for the thick smoke and follow your nose. Yum!

A customer waits for some barbecued chicken at a street stall.

THE FLAG OF JAMAICA

Jamaica's flag is black, green, and yellow. The yellow x-shaped cross makes two green and two black triangles. Green stands for hope and Jamaica's farms. Black stands for the country's past and the strength of the Jamaican people. Yellow stands for wealth and the beauty of sunshine.

FAST FACTS

FULL COUNTRY NAME: Jamaica

AREA: 4,471 square miles (11,580 square kilometers), or slightly smaller than Connecticut

MAIN LANDFORMS: the central limestone plateau; the coastal lowlands; the interior highlands; the Blue and Dry Harbor mountain ranges; the coast of the Caribbean Sea

MAJOR RIVERS: Black, Cobre, Grande, Minho, Nuevo, Plantain Garden, White, and Yallahs

ANIMALS AND THEIR HABITATS: bottle-nosed dolphins, hawksbill and other marine turtles (seacoast); bats, green parakeets, and mongooses (forests and woodlands); giant swallowtail butterflies (fields); Jamaican iguanas and lizards (dry limestone hills); crocodiles (rivers)

CAPITAL CITY: Kingston

OFFICIAL LANGUAGE: English

POPULATION: about 2,800,300

GLOSSARY

bargain: a talk between a buyer and a seller about the cost of an item. Bargaining ends when both sides agree on a price.

capital: the city where a country's government is located

continent: one of seven large areas of land. The continents are Africa, Antarctica, Asia, Australia, Europe, North America, and South America.

folktale: a timeless story told by word of mouth from grandparent to parent to child. Many folktales have been written down in books.

island: a piece of land surrounded by water

map: a drawing or chart of all or part of Earth or the sky

mountain: a part of Earth's surface that rises into the sky

mountain range: a series, or group, of mountains

patois: a form of English that also includes non-English words

port: a safe area on the shore of a body of water where ships can load and unload goods

tropical climate: a weather condition that is usually hot and in which lots of rain falls

TO LEARN MORE

BOOKS

Heinrichs, Ann. *Jamaica*. New York: Children's Press, 2008.
The author provides an introduction to the geography, culture, and people of Jamaica.

Krensky, Stephen. *Anansi and the Box of Stories*. Minneapolis: Millbrook Press, 2008.
This title shares both the facts and the fiction behind the folktale.

Stone, Vicky. *Countries of the World: Jamaica*. Washington, DC: National Geographic Society Childrens Books, 2008.
With outstanding photos, this book presents an in-depth view of Jamaica.

Zephaniah, Benjamin. *J is for Jamaica*. London: Francis Lincoln, 2006.
In this photographic alphabet book, the author introduces readers to the sights, sounds, and tastes of Jamaica.

WEBSITES

Jamaican Children's Songs
http://www.mamalisa.com
Learn the words and hear the melodies for Jamaican children's songs.

Kids Konnect-Jamaica
http://www.kidskonnect.com
Find additional information about Jamaica, its people, government, and history, and view a detailed map.

National Geographic
http://travel.nationalgeographic.com/places/maps/map_country_jamaica.html
See a slide show of Jamaican beaches. Watch a video about the history of the Maroons and one about the unique and dazzling birds, flowers, and butterflies on the island.

INDEX